Mountain,
Log,
Salt,
and Stone

Mountain, Log, Salt, and Stone

Laura Shovan

Winner of the Harriss Poetry Prize

Baltimore, Maryland

Library of Congress Control Number: 2010925257

ISBN 978-1-936328-02-4

CityLit Project is a 501(c)(3) Nonprofit Organization

Federal Tax ID Number: 20-0639118

Printed in the United States of America
First Edition

Cover and Book Design: Gregg Wilhelm
Book Design Assistance: Marisa Massaro,
Loyola University Maryland, '12
Author Photograph: Jennifer Lewis

"Summer, Veils" is a ghazal. The type is set in a smaller point size to
prevent the long lines from breaking.

c/o CityLit Project
120 S. Curley Street
Baltimore, MD 21224
410.274.5691
www.CityLitProject.org
info@citylitproject.org

Nurturing the culture of literature.

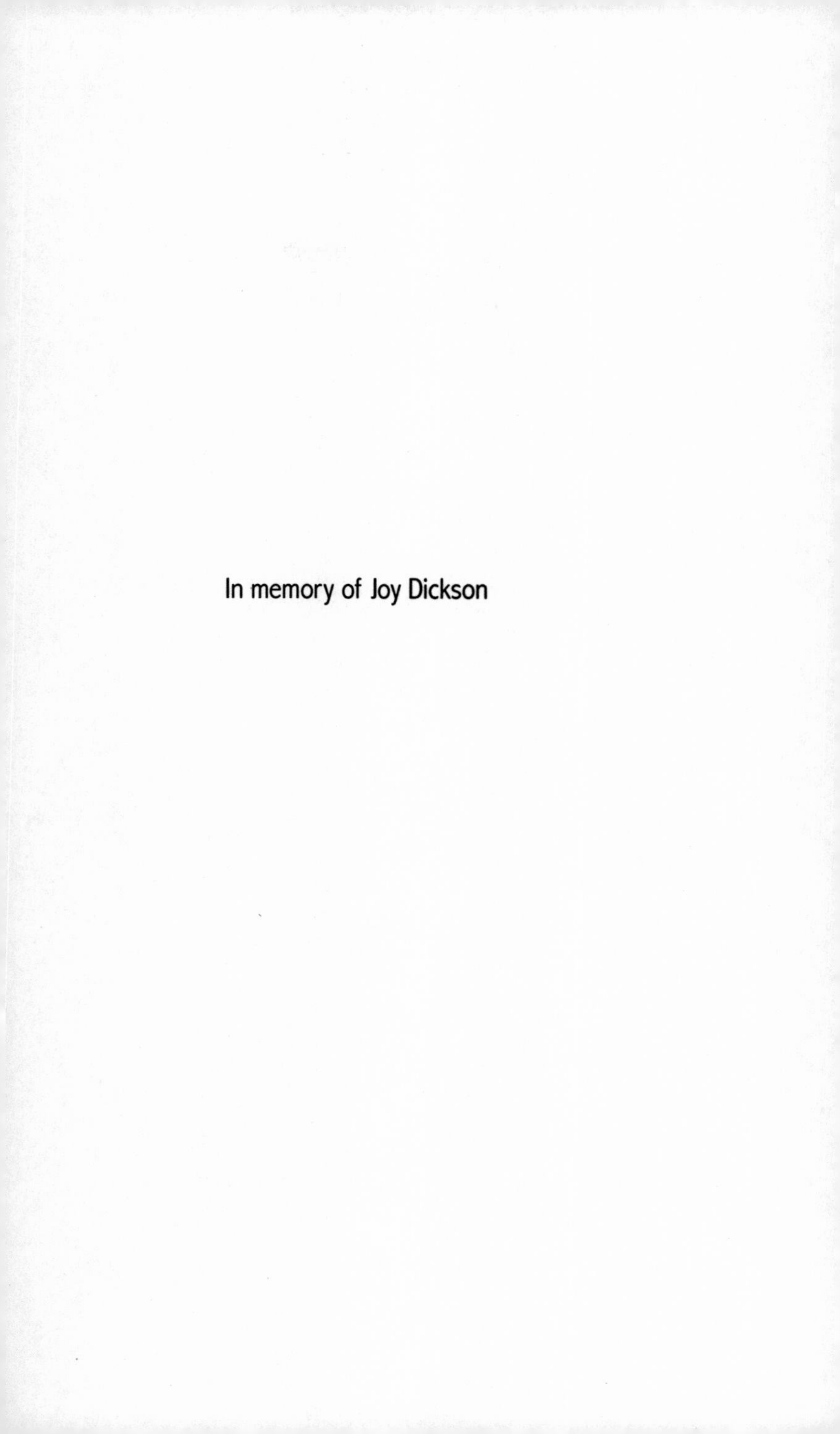

In memory of Joy Dickson

Table of Contents

Introduction

For more than thirty years Clarinda Harriss, professor and former chair of the department of English at Towson University, has taught her art to thousands of students, turning them into writing colleagues through the vivacious application of her kindness, enthusiasm, and professionalism, and by virtue of her wide expertise as poet, editor, and publisher. In establishing this prize in her name, CityLit Press honors an individual who honors writing and honors us all. It was my pleasure to choose the first winner of this annual competition. Despite many excellent manuscripts received from around the country, the thoroughly blinded selection of a winner did not prove to be that difficult; Laura Shovan, a writer in our own community, made it easy for me, combining within her person and within her art many of the same excellences that we find in the life and work of Clarinda Harriss.

Laura Shovan received her undergraduate degree from the Dramatic Writing Program at New York University's Tisch School of the Arts and obtained a master's degree in teaching from Montclair State University. After working as a high school teacher in New Jersey and as a program assistant with the Geraldine R. Dodge Foundation Program in Poetry, she studied with poets Maria Mazziotti Gillan, Madeline Tiger, Laura Boss, and Renee Ashley. She currently serves as an Artist-in-Education for the Maryland State Arts Council and has taught poetry and writing on behalf of CityLit Project and the Maryland Humanities Council to a wide variety of audiences. Laura's work for children has appeared in *Highlights* magazine, and her articles have appeared in the *Baltimore Sun*, *Baltimore Magazine*, and *Baltimore's Child*. Her poetry has been widely published in such magazines as *Lips*, *Paterson Literary Review*, *Global City*, and the *Little Patuxent Review*. Her work has twice received Honorable Mention for an Allen Ginsberg Poetry Award.

Laura's background in drama and television, journalism and teaching, childhood education and parenting, all clearly inform her poetry with an acute and dramatic attention to the details of everyday life. In her workshops with children and adults, she asks them "to stop and pay attention" because she feels that poetry begins with attentiveness and observation. For example, one day she heard her son say "tomorrow is going to be normal" and Laura turned this seemingly hopeful yet somehow chilling phrase into the kernel of a poem because she knows all too well how strange and abnormal the everyday world can be. In this she follows in the path of one of her artistic lodestars, the American poet William Stafford who, in his famous poem about what to do with a pregnant doe found dead at the roadside, "Traveling Through the Dark," is a master of this approach.

In her winning manuscript, "Mountain, Log, Salt, and Stone," Laura enlivens her quotidian subjects—the carpet rolls in the title poem, the pussy willow bud in "The Listening of Plants," and the dogwood petal in "Because We Were Rushing to Catch the Bus"—with a shrewd and powerful use of metaphor, a critical strategy all too often neglected in contemporary work. As Robert Frost so famously said, all of poetry is simply metaphor, meaning one thing and saying another. In the child's world, the log pile of carpet rolls become "mountains" to be scaled, her mother's accent "fits like an egg in her mouth," the pussy willow buds are "cat toes walking up a mottled branch," and, most wonderfully, the child inserts a bud into "the foyer of [her] ear." This is the word-surgeon's sure anatomical magic; so too the author's subtle command of poetic rhythm and a wide variety of poetic forms, from ghazal and free verse to triolets and prose poems.

Laura is also expert at transitioning her tenses and creating surprise in the reader through misdirection. In the opening poem of her manuscript, called "Driving Home From the Poetry Festival, 1996," her memory scrolls back from the title's journey to a drive her mother took years before. The second stanza begins "My mother, with me big in her belly" and suddenly we are made to experience the critical decision that saved their lives that night; a mysterious voice cries "Pull over." Whose voice is it, the internal voice of motherly intuition or the voice of the future poet *in utero*? The voice recurs with increasing urgency, transforming a memory poem into an *ars poetica* and successfully elaborating the complexity of William Stafford's model, the pregnant doe. There are many wonderful moments like this. From its zen-like title to the powerful conclusion of the very last poem, "Mountain, Log, Salt, and Stone" was the biggest and most imaginative submission in every way; it has now become a beautiful book.

Michael Salcman
Poet and Art Critic
Judge, Harriss Poetry Prize

Driving Home from the Poetry Festival, 1996

I would like to remember this night,
compel my mind to hoard sounds, images.
But Route 80 is featureless,
dark and nothing more.
I wish for some apparition,
a fire in the sky, the carcass
of an animal strewn across the road,
its blood flashing in snapshots.
Tonight words reached behind my eyes
like sea water, into my throat like desert air.
This night should be remembered.

My mother, with me big in her belly,
drove some other featureless highway,
the rest of the world home in bed.
A voice said, "Pull over."
And she did. Even though she was alone,
she listened to that voice,
and watched from the shoulder.
A darkened car hurtled the wrong way,
weaving the road toward her and me.
Tonight I say, speak to me, Voice,
so I will remember.

But I am closer to home with every mile,
knowing this drive will be forgotten,
not even hearing the radio drone.
Words burn in my mind.
There is no room for road,

or darkness, or music.
A voice I recognize now, as my own,
has whispered, *Mother, blood, belly.*
Carcass, car, desert.
These words anchor themselves just
long enough for me to write them here.

Red Crayon

I know the picture tells lies.
Not even the past is black and white.
My mother's hair is not gray.
She has dyed it blonde since the wedding.
She sits, wearing a silk dress.
The cut is western, sleeveless
short at the knee, but the fabric is foreign,
woven with dragons.
My father stands behind her,
his pink mouth closed.
They are spending the first year
of their marriage in Thailand.
They think there is enough room
between their two bodies
to imagine a daughter into existence.
But the photographer has posed them
so the space between them is as thin as rice paper.
I want to take a red crayon and rub it
on this rice paper my parents gave me.
I can rub the crayon over anything my father says,
make it disappear. I can write the things
my mother doesn't say, make them true.
I want to take a red crayon
and color my mother's face
red as the dragons on her dress should be.
I want to color outside the lines of her face,
red lines radiating around her head.
I want her to say she hates Thailand.

The food is too hot and a komodo dragon
lives under the house. I want her
to scratch his face and scream.
See how her words hang
in the gray space that envelops them?
Give me a red crayon.

Brother

"Ahmed and Mohamed Ibrahim—who had been joined at the top of the head—were separated...after neurosurgeons finished dividing the boys' venous systems and brains."
CNN, October 13, 2003

When did I become aware of my brother?
I can feel him only if we

stretch our arms overhead at once,
our fingers touch.

From above my eyes, I hear
laughing, crying, words not my own.

An echo self? Are there two of me?
No. Not me exactly, but me.

We are a continuous line, a human palindrome,
my twin doing a headstand on my skull

where people imagine light bulbs or dark clouds reside
I have myself again, but not myself.

Has God melded us, or has he never unmelded?
Those dancing mitochondria swaying apart

never stopped holding hands.
I have been given a word for the voice beyond my sight

and would like to face my brother.
I have never seen him, except at night

when I walk my feet up the crib slats
and he walks his feet up the other side.

If I raise my eyes almost to their lids
I can see—are they his toes?—moving.

And I have no sense of moving them.

Mountain, Log, Salt, and Stone

The mountain is taller than I,
halfway to the ceiling of our new living room.
This is how carpets are delivered,
piled in long, round rolls.
Put a penny in your mouth and you'll smell them:
acrid and heavy and new,
sour and exciting.
With my brother, I skate over the wood floor in socks,
try to crash the mountain of carpets.
Climb it and we are king and queen of a log pile.
We cannot fell or budge them.
These logs have no rot,
no rings to mark the fire or flood.
The disasters are all ahead of us.
When Dad is away we eat fast food,
French fries at the new stone hearth.
In two years our brother –
the child my mother is carrying –
will bang his chin on this stone
and nearly sever his tongue with his teeth.
There will be blood on the rug,
the salty taste of it in the air.
But tonight the scent of salt and oil
is good. Furniture is scant.

We gather on the floor around the fire.
The young painter stands by the window.
He has stopped rolling the walls
and joined us for dinner.

My mother is somewhere in the room.
The painter watches her.
He has dark hair and the youthful,
slender form my father has outgrown.
I watch the way his mouth moves
when he looks away from my mother.
The muscles of his back are taut with longing.
Less than ten years in this country,
her accent still fits like an egg in her mouth.
The painter is not the first to mistake
her round, elegant vowels for virtue.
I want her to take offense, to fire him.
But she is as kind and inattentive to him
as she is to anyone. Angry for her sake,
I begin to love my mother
with a viciousness the painter can't know.
I pull her to sit with us by the fire,
meals spread on our knees,
and let the warm salt dissolve on her tongue,
until it burns there like a pungent kiss.

Baby Yaga

What I loved about you, really, was your house.
We traveled the dirt road,
waiting for a glimpse of roof,
the familiar glint of sun on window.
The door, enormous and heavy,
belonged on a church.
Even I, the eldest, could not open it myself.

We explored the tiny room on the third floor
where I thought a crazy lady slept,
poked at the old gray parrot
who said your name in Grandpa's voice
and liked the taste of children's fingers,
warmed ourselves by the wide iron stove
that glowed charcoal all day long,
waiting, like the fairy tale,
for a plump and curious child.

Mornings, all three of us had tea in your bed.
The covers were filled with feathers.
Without your whalebone corset
you were powdery soft.
There were biscuits to eat.
Even Grandpa was friendly.

How easily we were trapped.
You pinched and prodded the other children,
who wisely kept their distance.
Your crooked pinky finger

scolds them in their memories:
our grandmother the witch.

We recognize you now,
we who you favored and fooled.
Your back is turned to us
and the old iron stove is burning.

The Listening of Plants

On the buffet where she kept her celadon dishes,
Mother placed a vase of pussy willows
hurried out of their branches.

The buds were cat toes walking up a mottled branch,
miniature koalas hanging on their eucalyptus
in a scattered line.

I snapped one off the twig and rolled the bud
on the flats of my thumb and finger,
its smoky gray coat how I imagined koala fur might feel.

I rubbed the willow bud along the bone of my jaw
wanting to know how a plant can wear animal skin.
It was too small, like touching nothing.

I splayed my hand along its curves,
felt the hairs rise in the divot of my palm.
I would have needed a sweater of willow to be satisfied.

Instead I slipped it into my ear. How did I know
a pussy willow was the right shape for the foyer of my ear,
long hall leading to the eardrum and the bones behind?

The bud rested there and I listened,
wanting to hear what it had to say
which was quiet, which was the muted listening of plants.

When I asked Mother to extract a pussy willow
from my ear, I couldn't explain its presence
how I listened and heard its secret.

In Early Spring

When color still arrests the eye,
a row of children's winter coats
slung over the playground fence.

Bright as tulips,
pairs of empty arms hang down.
They reach for earth, asking.

Each hood bows -- a line of prayer.
But the children?
Scattered like the milkweed to come,

nowhere.

Night Sounds

Petula was fourteen, lanky and bony-kneed. Her husband, twelve years older, sent her to summer camp. She moved in short bursts of energy, like the crickets we caught between our palms on the grassy hill. Their legs tickled. We wanted tiny bamboo cages to hold them. I was seventeen and had a boyfriend. I wondered: what is it to be a wife at fourteen? Petula could not be like my mother, keeping the house, the kids, the meals while Father worked. When I was a younger, watching my parents kiss, I couldn't squeeze myself between their legs. In love, at least, they were equals. Now, folded into my summer cot after lights out, I listened to the night sounds of the cabin. Girls breathed, sleeping, all around me. When I thought about my boyfriend, I envied Petula. Then I thought, "Does he make her?"

I saw him once. He was brown haired and bearded, soft. He watched his wife bounding between her friends like a worried father. Petula's parents lived in the Virginia hills, had a house filled with children. She had been plucked, with their blessing, from her home. I thought, "His house is like a bamboo cage." But now, I say he gave her the summer. That was a burst of kindness.

Aida

Newly married, I sit in the last rows of the Metropolitan Opera House with Sandra. In college, we took almost every class together. She may be a cynical New Yorker but she loves this spectacle. I admit the music is nice and maybe that's why I fall asleep while Aida sings to her lover from the cave where some power-crazed uncle or father has put her. How can her lover hear her from the cave? And I have to wonder how he fell in love with this enormous dumpling, princess or not. It must have been her money. I've drifted off listening to the aria. The lights darken. All I can see is a spotlight on the dumpling princess and the stars shining in the sky. The applause wakes me. Sandra says I have no culture. I feel kind of guilty. We take the subway to her parents' small house in Queens. Her mother brings me a washcloth and asks if I need anything else. Sandra says "Ma, we're fine." We stay up watching Letterman. I look at Sandra's photos of him, clipped from magazines, taped on the wall of her bedroom. I think, why am I here? It is the first time that my husband and I have slept apart. I am longing for our apartment, our bed. I have already stepped out of this circle of mothers, twin beds, and sleep over parties. I shake them off like the nubby pink bedspread Sandra's mother has put out especially for me.

Dear Sister, Unborn

At eight months, your elbows
were protrusions, your heartbeat
a murmur. I was two.
Resting my head on our mother's belly
I could not picture the shape of you.
I cannot picture my own child.
He is all backbone, his heart
a tiny red balloon.
I fear it might burst.

Knowing you, Sister, I see blood.
I look for signs of it on my under things,
for pink swirls in the toilet.
It is easier to imagine great clots
running down my thighs
than the sound of a baby
crying for me in the night,
than the sucking of a small mouth
at my breasts (which already hurt me).

Sister, that elbow in my face said,
"I am feverish to be free,"
not of her body, but of us all,
weary of life before you were born.
Our parents mourned.
Mother moved thickly
about the quiet house.
Even I, two years old,
felt the imprint of your loss.

Sister suicide, my child is invisible.
How could I hold him if he tried to escape?
I slice my palm in the kitchen
and know that he could rush out,
laughing, on the waves of my pulse.
Sister, I cannot force him to stay.
I can do nothing. Not even
make my heart stop beating,
like you.

Rites

I

What made us agree to this eight hour road trip,
this hotel room, unwelcoming even at 2 AM?
Was it the promise of sex, though we are synchronized
swimmers, diving exhausted into starched sheets?

At Saturday Mass, we watch a long-absent friend marry.
She is the first of us to wear an ivory dress.
She processes down the aisle. The gown forms a heart
on her back. Wedding guests dance with her for a dollar.

They lurch at her. She laughs and catches them in her arms.
The jilted boyfriend no one thought would come
is seated at our table, glowering at his fan-folded napkin
while the bride sings, "When I Fall in Love."

We leave early, walk the hotel hall with shoulders brushing.
But when we open the door, the sound
of bed hitting wall upstairs makes us giddy and sickened.
Friends of ours are in the room above.

We are quiet, as if the space around us
should not be disturbed. Even by a whisper.
That morning we see the bride in the hotel lobby
wearing a baby-blue dress my mother would call smart.

II

We are four hours closer to home
and take a chance on a road-side diner.
The special is turkey, beans, biscuits with gravy.
Sunday regulars arrive fresh from church.

An elderly man sits next to me at the picnic-style table.
He and I talk weddings. He asks about the ring,
the one you gave me. Back in the car,
we ask each other, "Wasn't that place strange?"

We are accustomed to all night delis, Chinese delivery.
But now I see we had been welcome there, expected even.
The diner folk saw what we could not:
this marriage, this child, this peace.

Leaving Home

The branches are bare
gray as they are every
winter

but this season their
reach is kinetic, their
fingers

enervate the blank sky.
I count trees in our yard.
Overhead

there are seven which throw
lattices of shade on the grass.
Not one

is rooted in our garden.
Coming over a hill, I face
a cloud

so blue and vast it is a mountain
against the sky. I ache for
such sights.

Thirty years I have lived in this town.
How long I've turned away,
forgetting.

I drive past an acre split into lots
and homes, remember its history:
long grass

and apple trees where we
escaped our fenced yards,
in-ground

swimming pools, woods
where the wild dogs lived
unnoticed.

Summer, Veils

Late summer an unexpected crop: beans veiled by hand-shaped leaves.
I lift one veil: green leaves, green vine, the bean a hidden lover.

Around me, threat of storm. Drums rattle the car stereo:
thunderous. A tenor sings angrily to his lover.

When the pond is full, a tranquil surface. Empty these long weeks,
it absorbs each drop of rain hungrily as a lover.

It is raining where you are. Here damp air lies against my skin,
a veil of moisture. Its touch is not unlike a lover's.

How am I like the mist? I am more tangible than air, yet
I might evaporate in the warm arms of a lover.

Take away my garden and the air and I am a woman
gasping only for ordinary things, not for her lover.

This is how it is: my car, my house, my son, myself, our pace
slow on this long road. You are the destination, my lover.

Peach Picking

Near the peach trees, a duck.
Orchard sentinel—waxy, ridged helmet of a head,
plume of white feathers lifting
each time it squawks.

It marches behind our small troop,
an outing of mothers and children,
herds us into the grassy path
between fruit trees.

In the moment I reach up
to pick fruit, the duck
snatches a half-eaten peach
from my son's palm.

It wants more—his fingers, arms.
I gather my son's small body,
Hoist him to my hip.
His arm is bruised black.

I am surprised when my own sneaker
kicks this bird pecking my ankles.
My friend opens her daughter's umbrella—
pink, plastic—to guard us.

Then we're in the van,
moving away from the orchard,
The children filled with questions.
Why was that duck mean

Mommy why did it bite me?
My friend and I shrug,
perplexed at the attack
by what should be tame.

At home, my son won't eat
the fruit until I scrape away
the ridged insides, that empty maze,
and revise his ruined day.

He wants his peaches smooth,
so I eat the hearts myself
and tell him this is where
the fruit is sweetest.

American Flamingo

Marsh wader
balanced on one leg,
like an apple tree in bloom,
webbed foot rooted to rock.
Marble eyes blue as the water
your boomerang beak
scoops for shrimp.

You are the color
of your dinner.
Your feathers might be
pale gray as the inside of a shell
or vacation sunburn pink.
Cotton candy, bubble gum,
hotel towel washed too many times.

Children ask me if you fly,
rise like a parasail over the beach.
Not that I've seen.
What did Audubon think
when he first saw a flock—
a shock to the corner of his eye—
of pink in summer sky?

Torii

After Rothko's *Untitled (Blue, Green, and Brown)*,1952

Torii at dusk,
I approach you.
What is beyond
your gate? Sleep,
dense as stone.

Triolet: A Visit to the Doctor of Herbal Medicine

She says, "You have the sadness in you."
She can see it in my dry, cracked hands.
My skin is raw with sorrow, it is true
what she says. "You have the sadness in you."
How can I hide it? Absence dries me through --
heart to knuckle-bones, I'm marked by its brands.
She says, "You have the sadness in you."
She can see it in my dry, cracked hands.

Wooly Bully

Driven inside by darkness and snow,
the three of us dance to "Woolly Bully."
We banish tables and chairs to corners,

crouch on the open floor like children
tracing animal prints in snow.
We dance a circle in each other's tracks—

father, mother, young howling.
We claw the air and grin.
Our teeth shine in the yellow light.

Outside, the animal stops to rest.
Its throat aches from cold.
It has seen a yellow light fall across the snow,

revealing its tracks. It wants to be caught.
It wants to be taken from the snow,
gathered in someone's arms, carried inside

a pet wrapped among our bodies.

An Absolute Vista

Our six year old climbed a snow bank at the back door
to walk and meet his father.
The snow was deep.
White erased everything—fences, sandbox.
Ground was something to imagine.

Why would he go?
His weight was too sleight
to puncture the icy crust with his boots.
Our son floated on the surface, a dark form
crawling away from the house.

Midway he stopped.
No one near but the wind, racing.

My husband left off sweeping pear branches,
strode deeply toward our child,
and lifted him off that shifting surface.
One body, they turned for home,
each step sinking to the good, solid ground.

Tomorrow Is Going to Be Normal

Walking home from the school bus, my son says,
"Tomorrow is going to be normal."
He speaks with the confidence of relief.
When every day is the same, he can breathe.

Each morning I tell myself,
Today, is the day—
I wait for the remarkable to land on my shoulder
or call me on the phone.

Sometimes it is a fortune written on the tag of my tea.
Sometimes it is a bird. Other days
I miss the quiet calling to attention.
I go to bed tired.

My son knows there is comfort in monotony.
Do I really want the phone to ring? It could be the lottery
or a hospital calling. He thinks my life is enough:
the mildness of the room when I am the only thing moving in it.

No. I must begin each day
wanting the next few hours to jolt me out of sameness.
He shakes his head. That we could be so different
we both find remarkable.

This Place Again

I. *What dreams may come*
When we have shuffled off this mortal coil,
Must give us pause
Hamlet, Act III, Scene I – William Shakespeare

There is a cup of light upstairs.
Julia's window shade is drawn
and light surrounds it.

I hesitate in the driveway.
The car still running, radio.
Inside I know

the dishes are done.
The children are not sleeping.
If I go in

they will flatten their books
on a thigh, against their chests,
and draw me upstairs with their calls.

What makes me pause, foot on brake?
Not the end of life, desire for death.
I am not a man contemplating his uselessness.

Children are my mortal coil.
But they know arms
are not enough to contain their mother.

If I go in, they will squeeze me
with all four limbs.
Their legs form an X on my back.

Pairs of fists press my shoulder blades.
In the driveway, I pause.
The life that goes on without me

is my own. I shuffle off tonight's companions,
conversations. Gauging who will want or need me,
I go inside.

II. *Among the rain and lights*
I saw the figure 5
"The Great Figure" – William Carlos Williams

Tonight the great 5
is Route 95
its glowing figure dangerously near,
a thread—drawing me north
to my first city.

I want to chase that golden 5
through Manhattan's wet streets
running, laughing. Let people stare.
I'll catch you, number 5.
Your siren is howling.

I'll jump aboard, feet on your golden scythe
hands gripping your top bar.
We'll wake them all,
crowds and children.
Poets rumbling: Awake, dark city.

III. *I see this place again*
This time the night as quiet
"At Our House" – William Stafford

Watching the silent house,
the stillness of its lights,
sometimes all that keeps me

from turning the car around
is the breath borne gently on the air,
and how it would catch if I weren't there.

Because We Were Rushing to Catch the Bus

we did not notice the rain.
Too late for umbrellas,
we ran down the sidewalk,
wishing we'd taken the car.

Because we ran
under rain soaked trees,
the children's heads were damp
when I kissed them at the corner.

Because the children were gone,
I walked home alone.
Dishes in the sink
waiting.

Because of the dishes
I bent my head
before the kitchen window.
A petal fell from my hair—

a pink thumbprint against metal,
pink against the gray day,
pink against the absence of children.
It shook me awake.

Because we were rushing to catch the bus
I carried beauty, unknowing.

Credits

"Aida," with the title, "Newly Married," *Lips*

"American Flamingo," *Gunpowder Review*

"Baba Yaga," *Paterson Literary Review*

"Because We Were Rushing to Catch the Bus," *Joyful!*

"Brother," *Little Patuxent Review* and *New Lines from the Old Line State: An Anthology of Maryland Writers*

"Dear Sister, Unborn," *Paterson Literary Review* and *Global City Review*

"Driving Home from the Poetry Festival, 1996," *Paterson Literary Review* and *Little Patuxent Review*

"In Early Spring," *Gunpowder Review*

"The Listening of Plants," *Little Patuxent Review*

"Mountain, Log, Salt, and Stone," *Jewish Women's Literary Annual* and *New Lines from the Old Line State: An Anthology of Maryland Writers*

"Night Sounds," *Jewish Women's Literary Annual*

"Red Crayon," *Paterson Literary Review*

"Rites," *Paterson Literary Review*

"Wooly Bully," *Little Patuxent Review*

Acknowledgments

Many of these poems were written with the encouragement and support of the Dodge Poetry Program and Dodge Poets Maria Mazziotti Gillan, Madeline Tiger, Renée Ashley, and Laura Boss.

My compatriots in poetry Mary Florio, Jean Meyers, Michael Z Murphy, and Margaret Valentine helped get me started, sent me off into the world, and still consider me an honorary HillPoet.

Thanks to the Maryland State Arts Council, CityLit Project, Kendra Kopelke, and especially Michael Salcman for his mentorship.

Among my teachers are the children I work with, both in schools and at home. Special thanks to Robbie and Julia. And my deepest gratitude to my husband Rob.

About the Poet

Laura Shovan grew up in New Jersey. She is an honors graduate of the Dramatic Writing Program at New York University's Tisch School of the Arts.

During her first career as a high school English teacher, Laura was active in the Geraldine R. Dodge Foundation's Poetry Program, studying with Maria Mazziotti Gillan, Madeline Tiger, Renee Ashley, and Laura Boss. Laura coordinated poetry readings by award-winning teens at the 1996 and 1998 Dodge Poetry Festivals. Since 2002, Laura has been an Artist-in-Education for the Maryland State Arts Council, leading poetry workshops for school children.

She has taught for the Maryland Humanities Council's "Totally Ekphrastic: Picturing America through Poetry" program, CityLit Project's "Write Here, Write Now" workshops, and the G/T Summer Institutes in Howard County, Maryland.

Laura has written articles and essays about education, parenting, learning disabilities, and the arts for *Baltimore's Child*, the *Baltimore Sun*, and other publications. Her poetry has appeared in many journals, including the *Global City Review*, *Jewish Women's Literary Annual*, *Lips*, *Little Patuxent Review*, and *Paterson Literary Review*. She has earned two Allen Ginsberg Poetry Awards honorable mentions.

Laura is actively involved in the Society of Children's Book Writers and Illustrators (SCBWI), with credits in *Highlights! for Children* and *Shoofly* audio magazine. She lives in Howard County, Maryland, with her husband and two children.

Mountain, Log, Salt, and Stone is her first chapbook.

The Harriss Poetry Prize

Launched in 2009, the Harriss Poetry Prize is named in honor of Clarinda Harriss, eminent Baltimore poet, publisher, and professor of English at Towson University. Harriss, educated at Johns Hopkins University and Goucher College, is a widely published, award-winning poet and she serves as editor/director of BrickHouse Books, Maryland's oldest literary press.

2009 Judge: Michael Salcman

For complete guidelines, please go to www.citylitproject.org and click on "CityLit Press." Send entry fee, manuscript with table of contents, acknowledgments, and two coversheets (one with name, title, mailing address, daytime phone, and email address and one with *title only*) to:

Harriss Poetry Prize
CityLit Press
c/o CityLit Project
120 S. Curley Street
Baltimore, MD 21224

Annual submission deadline is October 1 (postmarked).

CityLit Press's mission is to provide a venue for writers who might otherwise be overlooked by larger publishers due to the literary quality or regional focus of their projects. It is the imprint of nonprofit CityLit Project, founded in Baltimore in 2004.

CityLit nurtures the culture of literature in Baltimore and throughout Maryland by creating enthusiasm for literature, building a community of avid readers and writers, and opening opportunities for young people and diverse audiences to embrace the literary arts.

Thank you to our major supporters: the Maryland State Arts Council, the Baltimore Office of Promotion and The Arts, and the Baltimore Community Foundation. More information and documentation is available at www.guidestar.org.

Additional support is provided by individual contributors. Financial support is vital for sustaining the on-going work of the organization. Secure, on-line donations can by made at our web site, click on "Donate."

CityLit is a member of the Greater Baltimore Cultural Alliance, the Maryland Association of Nonprofit Organizations, and the Writers' Conferences and Centers division of the Association of Writers and Writing Programs (AWP).

For submission guidelines, information about CityLit Press's poetry chapbook contests, and all the programs and services offered by CityLit, please visit www.citylitproject.org.

Nurturing the culture of literature.

CPSIA information can be obtained
at www.ICGtesting.com
Printed in the USA
FFOW04n0959250216
21819FF